j 794.85 Minecraft 2018
Schwartz, Heather E.
The world of Minecraft /
9781512483130

4/2018

P9-DCG-350

Searchlight BOOKS™

The World of Gaming

The World of Minecraft

Hamilton East Public Library
1 Library Plaza
Noblesville, IN 46060

Heather E. Schwartz

Lerner Publications ◆ Minneapolis

This book is dedicated to Nolan Schwartz, my brilliant son with a talent for tech and a vast knowledge of *Minecraft* in particular. Thank you for letting me mine your brain for info to include in this book!

Copyright © 2018 by Lerner Publishing Group, Inc.

All rights reserved. International copyright secured. No part of this book may be reproduced, stored in a retrieval system, or transmitted in any form or by any means—electronic, mechanical, photocopying, recording, or otherwise—without the prior written permission of Lerner Publishing Group, Inc., except for the inclusion of brief quotations in an acknowledged review.

Lerner Publications Company
A division of Lerner Publishing Group, Inc.
241 First Avenue North
Minneapolis, MN 55401 USA

For reading levels and more information, look up this title at www.lernerbooks.com.

Library of Congress Cataloging-in-Publication Data

The Cataloging-in-Publication Data for *The World of Minecraft* is on file at the Library of Congress.
ISBN 978-1-5124-8313-0 (lib. bdg.)
ISBN 978-1-5415-1198-9 (pbk.)
ISBN 978-1-5124-8317-8 (EB pdf)

LC record available at https://lccn.loc.gov/2017038563

Manufactured in the United States of America
1-43330-33150-10/4/2017

Contents

Chapter 1

MINING AND CRAFTING

You run down a hill and cross a river in the world of *Minecraft*. After collecting some wood, you create planks to make a crafting table. On the table, you craft a pickax. The tool will come in handy when you search a cave for coal to make a torch.

Every step in *Minecraft* must be carefully planned if you want to survive. Will you make it through the night?

A crafting table is used to make more complex items such as tools and weapons.

Before creating *Minecraft*, Markus "Notch" Persson worked for the company that made the game *Candy Crush*.

Minecraft fans play in a vast world with almost unlimited freedom to be creative. But would you believe that the basic elements of *Minecraft* were created in only a few days? A Swedish game developer named Markus "Notch" Persson coded the game that quickly in 2009. He was in a hurry because he wanted to move on to other games. He had no idea the one he'd just made would become a smash hit.

When Persson finished creating *Minecraft*, he decided to post it online. He got his first response from a gamer in about eight minutes. Over the next twenty-four hours, players posted dozens of comments about the game. Gamers were excited about *Minecraft*.

Chatting with players helped Persson decide on a name for the game. At first, it was called *Minecraft: Order of the Stone*. He later shortened it to *Minecraft*.

GAMERS CAN PLAY *MINECRAFT* ALONE OR ONLINE WITH FRIENDS.

Meet Markus "Notch" Persson

Markus "Notch" Persson was obsessed with Lego toys as a young boy. Putting the colored blocks together to build something is similar to coding. He got his first computer, a Commodore 128, when he was seven years old. He soon started coding on the computer.

Putting blocks together to form a building is similar to the way people put instructions together to code a video game.

There are many different ways to play *Minecraft*, which helps it appeal to gamers of all ages.

Building a Business

The excitement about *Minecraft* encouraged Persson to start his own gaming company. He joined with friend and fellow game developer Jakob Porser. They called their company Mojang.

Persson kept chatting with gamers and making changes to *Minecraft* based on their suggestions. The game spread like wildfire. By the middle of 2010, people were buying four hundred copies of *Minecraft* every day. Each download cost six dollars. That's some serious cash!

Minecraft had gone viral, so Mojang didn't need to spend much money on advertising. Sales hit one million copies in January 2011. When Mojang released *Minecraft: Xbox 360 Edition*, the game sold more than a million copies in the first week.

By 2014, *Minecraft: Xbox 360 Edition* had sold more than twelve million copies.

Chapter 2

A WORLD OF CHOICES

Gamers call *Minecraft* a sandbox game. Do you know why? It's because you can build almost anything there. Of course, you don't really use sand. You use materials such as wood and stone that you find in the game.

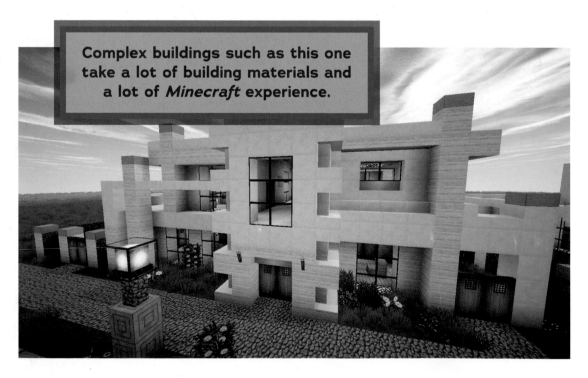

Complex buildings such as this one take a lot of building materials and a lot of *Minecraft* experience.

Players can make choices about how Steve (*left*) and Alex look, such as different outfits and hair color.

How do you start playing *Minecraft*? That's easy. You just choose your character.

For a long time, a character named Steve was the only free default character option. Mojang wanted gamers to have another choice. In 2015, the company introduced Alex, a female character.

The Modes of *Minecraft*

One way to play *Minecraft* is called Survival mode. Gamers gather items, build structures, find food, and craft tools. They also have to avoid getting killed by monsters that come out at night, called mobs.

ZOMBIES, SKELETONS, AND CREEPERS ARE THREE OF THE MONSTERS TO AVOID AT NIGHT.

▼

In Survival mode, players must manage their health and make sure they have enough food.

Minecraft has other modes too. Some gamers like Hardcore mode. It's more difficult than Survival and doesn't give gamers a second chance. If their characters die, it's game over. Spectator mode allows gamers to roam without interacting with the world. Creative mode lets players focus on crafting and building. Players get unlimited building materials without even searching for them.

Meet a Video Game Programmer

Have you ever wondered how video games are made? The answer is programming, or coding. Video game programmers write code that computers use to run a game's graphics, sounds, and gameplay. Hundreds of programming languages exist, including Java. That's the language Persson used to code *Minecraft*.

Kurt J. Mac's long walk appeared in *Guinness World Records*.

The *Minecraft* world is much larger than Earth. Players call the ends of the game the Far Lands. Gamer Kurt J. Mac's *Minecraft* character started walking across the game's world in 2011. By 2015, he'd traveled farther than any other player, more than 1,303 miles (2,097 km). At that pace, Mac's character could walk for years before he reached the Far Lands.

Minecraft player Duncan Parcells said Titan City was inspired by New York City.

Titan City

With so much to explore and so many ways to play, it's no wonder that fifty-five million gamers enjoy *Minecraft* each month. One of the game's biggest fans is former art student Duncan Parcells. From 2012 to 2014, he built a huge *Minecraft* community called Titan City.

Parcells spent about five hours each week on his creation. When Titan City was finally finished, it had ninety-six buildings. Parcells had used 4.5 million *Minecraft* blocks to create the city.

Chapter 3

MINING FOR MORE

Gamers love *Minecraft*, and they buy tons of merchandise to prove it. Stuffed toys, T-shirts, hoodies, hats, action figures, and books are all big sellers. There's a Lego *Minecraft* set with sixteen hundred pieces. People even buy life-size toy swords with that famous *Minecraft* look.

Stuffed *Minecraft* critters have the same boxy look they have in the game.

Dressing up as a video game character is called cosplay.

Fans also like to get together with fellow *Minecraft* players. In 2010, gamers met at MinecraftCon in Bellevue, Washington. Between thirty and fifty people gathered for the event.

MinecraftCon soon became MineCon, and it's more popular than ever. In 2016, thousands of fans showed up for MineCon at the Anaheim Convention Center in California. They dressed up as *Minecraft* characters and took part in fun and informative events.

Many fans have been inspired to take the game's creativity from the screen to the real world. A scientist named Mark Cheverton wrote a series of novels set in the world of *Minecraft*. The books have more than a million copies in print. Daniel Middleton created a popular YouTube channel focused on *Minecraft*. As DanTDM (The Diamond Minecart), he records his adventures in the game.

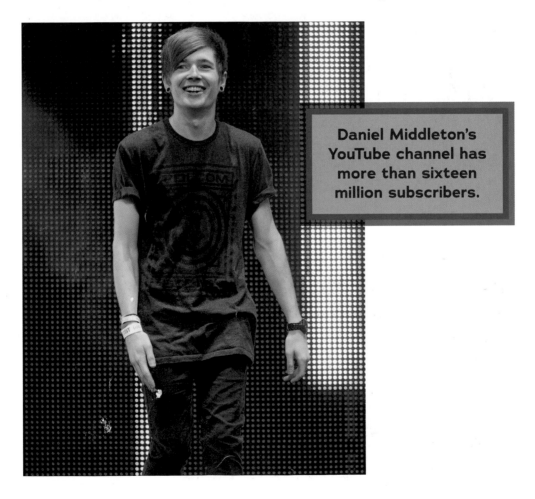

Daniel Middleton's YouTube channel has more than sixteen million subscribers.

Minecraft: Story Mode players change the game's story by reacting to different situations.

Okay, I'll work for you. X ⬩ B I'll never join you!

Story-Mode Spinoff

Minecraft: Story Mode is another way fans can get into the game. It's a series of stories that people can watch and play. As players watch, the game periodically offers choices on the screen. Fans choose an option to decide how the story will go from there.

Meet an Animator

Animators are artists who bring characters and stories to life in TV shows, movies, and—you guessed it—video games. Animators usually love art, computers, or both. They study subjects such as computer graphics and fine arts.

Chapter 4

MINECRAFT MOVES FORWARD

In 2014, Persson sent a surprising message on Twitter. He asked if anyone wanted to buy his portion of Mojang. The creator of *Minecraft* was ready to leave his company and the game behind. He wanted to work on new projects.

Persson made a lot of money selling Mojang. He bought this house in Beverly Hills, California, in 2014 for $70 million.

Microsoft is one of the world's most successful companies, and it helped *Minecraft* become even more popular.

Executives at the technology company Microsoft saw Persson's message. They wanted to buy Mojang, and they had the money to do it. Microsoft paid $2.5 billion for the gaming company in 2014.

New ownership didn't harm *Minecraft*'s popularity. By 2016, sales reached 107 million copies. That made it the second-best-selling video game of all time. About 53,000 copies of Minecraft continue to sell each day.

Meet Alexey Pajitnov

You probably don't know the name Alexey Pajitnov, but you may know his game. He's the creator of *Tetris*, the top-selling video game ever.

When Pajitnov coded *Tetris* in 1984, he wanted to test the limits of computers. He also wanted to show people that computers could be fun. What a success!

Block by Block helps improve
cities around the world.

A Real Game Changer

Mojang is helping people in developing countries use
Minecraft to benefit their communities. People can use
the game to plan parks, roads, and other real-life projects.
In 2012, Mojang created Block by Block. The charity
raises money to build those projects.

Minecraft: Education Edition is designed for students to work in teams or together with their whole class.

Minecraft has even found its way into schools, making learning fun for students. *Minecraft: Education Edition* launched in 2016. It has lesson plans about math, science, and other subjects. Students can even use the game to learn how to write code.

Minecraft is a superfun game. But can you imagine a movie about it? You don't have to imagine. *Minecraft: The Movie* is set to open on the big screen in theaters across the country in 2019. *Minecraft* fans can't wait to see their favorite game brought to life as a film!

MANY MOVIES BASED ON VIDEO GAMES, SUCH AS *THE ANGRY BIRDS MOVIE* IN 2016, HAVE BEEN SUCCESSFUL.

▼

Endless Potential

How does a video game that was created in just days become so popular? *Minecraft* did it by capturing people's imaginations. Fans are more than just players in this digital world. They're part of its creation.

Persson decided to move on to new challenges. But *Minecraft*'s fans will keep playing, building, and creating for years to come. In the world of *Minecraft*, the options are endless.

Minecraft players can build almost anything they can imagine.

Bonus Points

- The word *mojang* means "gadget" in Swedish.

- Between April and May 2013, gamers spent a total of one billion hours playing *Minecraft: Xbox 360 Edition*. That's about 114,000 years!

- What happens to kids who grow up playing video games? They become adult gamers! The average gamer is thirty-five years old.

Glossary

code: create instructions for a computer

default: an option used when no other option is available or has been selected

download: to transfer files from one computer to another

gamer: a person who plays video games

merchandise: items that are bought and sold

mob: short for mobile. In Minecraft, mobs are mobile creatures, or creatures that move freely.

mode: the rules and settings of a game. Some games have different modes that affect how the game is played.

viral: spreading very quickly to many people

Learn More about Video Games

Books

Cornell, Kari. Minecraft *Creator Markus "Notch" Persson*. Minneapolis: Lerner Publications, 2016. Learn how Markus "Notch" Persson's love of computers and design helped him create *Minecraft*.

Keppeler, Jill. *The Inventors of Minecraft: Markus "Notch" Persson and His Coding Team*. New York: PowerKids, 2018. Find out more about Markus "Notch" Persson and the team that made *Minecraft* a worldwide sensation.

Milton, Stephanie. Minecraft *Combat Handbook*. New York: Scholastic, 2015. Discover how to defend yourself, defeat your enemies, and survive in the world of *Minecraft*.

Websites

Code.org
https://code.org/student
Find a course and learn to code computer games on your own.

KidzSearch: *Minecraft*
https://wiki.kidzsearch.com/wiki/Minecraft
This website is full of information about *Minecraft*'s modes, mobs, and much more.

Minecraft Official Site
https://minecraft.net/en-us
Get all the *Minecraft* info you need straight from the official source.

Index

Photo Acknowledgments

Image acknowledgements: Minecraft screenshots, pp. 4, 6, 11, 12, 13; Paul Hennessy/Polaris/Newscom, p. 5; iStock.com/AngiePhoto, p. 7; Matthew Tostevin/Reuters/Newscom, p. 8; Christian Petersen/Getty Images, p. 9; Etereui/Pixabay CC0, p. 10; Ints Kalnins/Reuters/Newscom, p. 14; James Ellerker/Photoshot/Newscom, p. 15; courtesy of Duncan Parcells, p. 16; Gabe Ginsberg/FilmMagic/Getty Images, p. 17; Yui Mok/PA Images/Alamy Stock Photo, p. 18; Justin Tallis/AFP/Getty Images, p. 19; *Minecraft: Story Mode* S2 E3/Telltale Games, p. 20; Pius Utomi Ekpei/AFP/Getty Images, p. 21; CelebrityHomePhotos/Newscom, p. 22; Roberto Machado Noa/LightRocket/Getty Images, p. 23; Francois Lo Presti/AFP/Getty Images, p. 24; Games for Change/flickr.com (CC BY-ND 2.0), p. 25; *Minecraft: Education Edition*, p. 26; © Columbia Pictures/Courtesy Everett Collection, p. 27; Shadowman39/Flickr (CC BY 2.0), p. 28.

Cover: Christian Petersen/Getty Images.

Main body text set in Adrianna Regular 14/20.
Typeface provided by Chank.